Poetic Inspirations

My Life in Poetry

ORIGINAL POETRY BY:

MELODY D. VELEZ-ORTEGA

DEDICATION

This book is dedicated to my husband and children. It's a collection of my deepest thoughts and emotions and I am happy to share it with the world. I hope my family, friends and fans will learn a little bit more about who I am as an individual. They may even learn a little bit more about who they are by seeing they are not alone in their thoughts and feelings.

Feel free to share your thoughts with me via email and/or social media.
Open dialogue is encouraged!

Email: mylifeinpoetrymv@gmail.com

Instagram and Twitter: @mylifeinpoetrymv

v

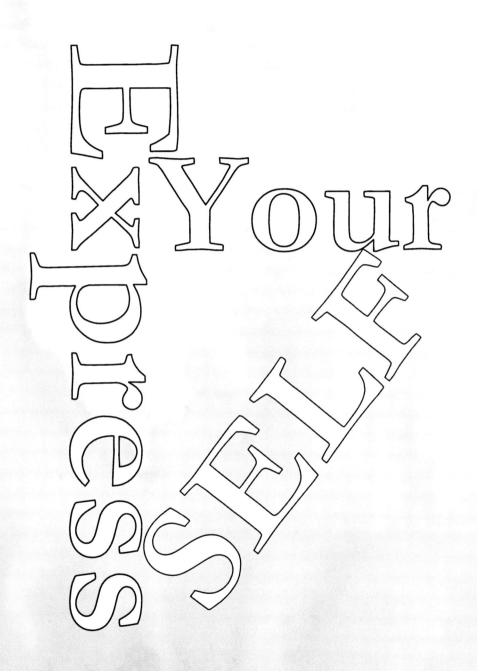

ACKNOWLEDGMENTS

I WANT TO TAKE A MINUTE AND THANK EVERYONE I'VE MET ALONG MY PATH FOR INSPIRING ME TO BE WHO I AM. ESPECIALLY MY HUSBAND, AND MY WONDERFUL CHILDREN AND STEPCHILDREN. WITHOUT THEM, I WOULDN'T HAVE THE PASSION TO WRITE AGAIN. ALL MY EXPERIENCES IN LIFE HAVE MADE ME THE STRONG WOMAN I AM TODAY. FLAWS AND ALL.

From A Child's Eye

Mommy I watch You
Daddy I see
You work hard and are tired
All to support me

But what about me

I'm just a child,
Who wants to play
I don't really understand why
You're busy everyday

I want your attention
Don't you see and hear me?
I think you both need an intervention
How blind can you be?

You're doing your best
I know that you try
But you really don't understand
the reasons I cry

Please take a little time
For you and for me
That is the key
To a happy family

Momma Why?

Why were you so distant?
Did you abandon your motherly instincts?
You always made me cry
Many times, I wanted to die
You never listened; you always fought
But still it was your love that I sought

Momma Why?

For years I resented you
I ran away a lot too
I felt scared and alone
I didn't know what to do

Momma Why?

Please help me understand
Why you chose to raise your hands
It hurt, emotionally and physically
'Till this day it affects me mentally

Momma Why?

Okay Momma,
Now I see...
You were not okay mentally
You were abused and treated bad
That's why you were always so sad
Repeating history is all you knew
You were actually a victim too

I love You Momma!

An Addicts Monologue

(WRITTEN FROM MY MOTHER'S PERSPECTIVE)

I SELF-INFLICT DISEASE,
TO FEED MY BODY WHAT IT NEEDS
I LIE, I CHEAT, I KNOW NO DEFEAT
I SMOKE IT, I SWALLOW IT, I EVEN SNORT
I DO DRUGS OF ANY SORT

MY FAMILY, I LOVE THEM
BUT IT'S ALL ABOUT ME
IT'S THE EUPHORIA I FEEL WITHIN MY MIND
ABUSING OF DRUGS OF EVERY KIND

PROBLEMS DISINTEGRATE AS QUICKLY AS THEY APPEAR
I FEEL AS THOUGH THERE IS NOTHING TO FEAR

I ABUSE MY FAMILY MENTALLY AND PHYSICALLY
I DESTROY WHAT'S LEFT OF THEIR MENTAL STABILITY

IF PEOPLE KNEW ALL THE PAIN I'VE ENDURED,
I THINK THEY WOULD UNDERSTAND WHY I'M NOT ME
ANYMORE

I'VE BEEN LIED TO, I'VE BEEN HURT
AND MOST MY LIFE TREATED LIKE DIRT
ABUSED BOTH PHYSICALLY AND EMOTIONALLY
THE SUFFERING I ENDURED RUINED ME MENTALLY

THE CYCLE OF LIFE CLAIMS ANOTHER SOUL
IT'S ALMOST IMPOSSIBLE FOR ME TO FEEL WHOLE
MY LIFE IS FALLING APART, BUT WHO THE HELL CARES
I'LL CONTINUE TO LIVE IN MY WORLD
WHILE EVERYONE CHOOSES TO REMAIN UNAWARE

Depression

There are times in my life I'm such a Mess
Feeling so stressed, moody and depressed
I wake up feeling so scared,
so fatigued, Man, I could care less

It's tough to shake the emptiness
The emptiness I feel inside,
So many thoughts are in my head
So many that they all collide

What do I do?
Where do I go?
Do I get out of bed?
The answer is no
What is wrong with me?
Does anybody see?
The deep sadness that lives inside me.

Why am I crying?
I'm tired of fighting
I need help,
I need love,
I need answers from above

Don't ask me what's wrong
It just saddens me more
I cry, and cry 'till my insides are sore

Hold me,
Love me,
Kiss me,
Console me
Even if just for a moment

Dilemmas

Dilemmas of the mind
Dilemmas of the soul
Too many problems for one person to hold

Situations of past, born again new
Situations with no solutions
What could one do?

Problematic individuals engulfing your mind
Almost impossible to leave problems behind

Like a disease devouring you mentally
Perhaps these issues have meaning & are meant to be

No choice but to accept the hand dealt to you
These are the things that people must live through

How does one learn to let go?
With negativity so strong, I guess one will never know

I've learned to live with the auras around me
The light and the darkness constantly surrounding
me

Although many times these auras are uncooperative
I look to the future and strive to stay positive

Don't Despair

Ladies don't despair.

There are still people who care.

Don't let harassment by others be your downfall

Even when you feel your back is to the wall.

Be Strong, stay alive,

and keep your mind energized.

Your life will be better than you realized.

There are ways to get through this,

Believe me, I know.

I've fought and I've cried,

and it has helped me to grow.

If you feel depressed or scared,

Ladies don't despair.

If you feel you have everything to lose,

Whatever you do, break those feelings loose.

Keep your head up; don't get fed up.

Ladies don't despair.

Keep your mind and spirit aware.

Even when you feel your heart is about to tear,

Always remember there is someone who cares.

What's Unique About Me

What's unique about me?
Is it hard to see?
Is it my Personality?
Or my originality?

My strength
My will, my exceptional skills?
Is it my knowledge,
That I acquired in college?

Is it my patience, my kindness?
The ability to overlook others faults with blindness.
Is it the children I birthed?
Who see all I'm worth?

Is it the ability to see what no one else could?
To laugh and to cry when no one else would?
Is it my generosity? my simplicity?
My artistic ability?
All of which are a great gift to me

All of these things are a part of my being
And certainly, all have an important meaning
The things about me that stand out the most,
Are my determination to strive and my will to survive

I've learned to stay strong during years of heartache
and pain
And the one thing I've learned
is that it has not been in vain.
I am extremely proud of my curriculum vitae
All of this made me the woman I am today

New Beginnings

The waking of a new day,
All my problems are out of my way

Finally walking a straight line
About to start a journey, that's all mine

No more rules and regulations
My life now follows my own stipulations

Finally, free to do as I please
To be able to raise my children with ease

With more responsibilities still to come
It's strange, but I actually welcome them

Time to leave the past behind,
And live my life with some peace of mind

Humanity

What is this world coming to?

Rage
Deception
Betrayal
Misconceptions
Homicide

Is this the new age of genocide?

Humanity is quickly diminishing
A festering ulcer created by man which is infinitely
increasing

An economy which is failing financially
Due to our failure to deal with deficits rationally

Parent's killing children
Children killing each other
Will this world ever recover?

Races at war with each other
Senseless deaths have life's meaning outnumbered

Why do we do this? What is it for?
Is it for power or to even a score?

There must be a point in reality
Where we can see past money, race and legalities
To recover what remains of our world's humanity
And live with an abundance of peace, not brutality

Society's Pain

The trouble with society today,
Is the lack of compassion in every way.
The senseless crime waves at a rise,
All the pollution in the skies.

The violence, the deceit for all to see.
What has society become?
How did we let this be?

The anger, the pain and the sadness,
How much longer can we endure this madness?

Senseless deaths and discriminatory acts,
Judging each other without all the facts.

The pain and the struggles that people endure,
What more does the future have in store?

Struggles

When we were children
We took life for granted
We said, "I can't wait to grow up!"
And later recanted

Work, work, work
Never any time to play
Hustling to survive
Day after day

Work hard to make money
Money we never see
We work to pay bills
And wish money grew on trees

Our blood, sweat and tears
are what we are taught to give
While we dream of our childhood
that we want to relive

If Only

If only you knew...
Then you won't...
But you don't.

If only you felt...
What I felt...
Then you'd melt.

If only you could understand what I think...
Then maybe you'd hold my hand
When my nerves are on the brink

Feelings

I feel torn, abused and always used
All emotions I feel cannot be excused
Ashamed, to blame
Feelings I cannot tame
So sad, that I feel like a pawn in a game

Can't run, can't hide,
Can't escape from what's real
The realization that it's wrong what I feel
Can't stop it, can't block it
Can't lie to my gut

I guess that's why my life is screwed up

Ghost Pain

I'M TIRED
IN PAIN
IN MY BACK
IN MY CHEST
IN MY HEART
THROUGH MY VEINS

THE SWELLING
THE CRAMPING
THE PAIN I ENDURE
THE DOCTORS FIND NOTHING
NO DIAGNOSIS, NO CURE

IS IT ALL IN MY MIND?
THE PAIN THEY CAN'T FIND
IT MUST BE THIS DAILY GRIND
THAT HAS MY GHOST PAINS UNDEFINED

It's Been Six Years

It's been six years,
You still don't know me.

It's been six years,
Together, but still lonely.

It's been six years,
And still much uncertainty.

It's been six years,
Of you thinking you love me.

It's been six years,
Full of doubt and insecurity.

It's been six years,
Of your lack of trust in me.

It's been six years,
Full of your lies and infidelities.

It's been six years,
You still don't see the hurt in me.

It's been six years,
You're on a different page then me.

Can't you feel my suffering?
I can't continue waiting.
I can't continue wondering.
Each year my love is fading.

What more will it take?
I stuck by you; what a mistake.
I've lost sight of who I am.
Stop be a stranger and be my man.

Lost Love

My love, my life, my everything,
Until you gave that other girl my ring
You told me that our love would be forever
And then I felt the worst pain ever

You told me you looked into her eyes
And you felt love instantly
That's when I realized our love would never be

She showed you things I never could
And unlike me she understood
She catered to your every demand
She was there to hold your hand

All the times I held you close in my arms
You said that you would never cause me harm
You took my heart and trampled it
Then picked it up and proceeded to stab it

I lied to my instincts,
believed they weren't true
But I guess you wanted a mother,
And I'm not here to cradle you

I put up with all your selfish demands
The verbal and physical abuse you inflicted
because you thought you were a man

I realize now I am happy you left,
I am forever grateful for her theft.
I thought I suffered a lost love
But a new me emerged
That was a gift from above

Venom

You are a Mother@#$% Bastard
You have me feeling Manic
You walk around thinking you're the don
But you don't realize, you just lost one

You think you can do what you please
Don't come crawling on your knees
Stay with that dirty ass skeeze
Staying out all night
You think that's alright
Well asshole I put up a good fight
This Bitch right here can find another lover
Then all you'll be left with is a love hangover

Remember what you did to me
And maybe then you'll see
Through all the years, I gave you everything

Keep messing with me,
You'll feel the scorpion sting
I'm running ragged
Got my mind feeling Jagged
You maggot
You think you have it good?
All you'll ever be is a loser in the hood

You're going to find yourself, by yourself
Singing another sad love song
Knowing that you did wrong

You really thought you had a Bitch Tamed
You better learn my Motherf@#$% name
A Bitch like me has been on to all your games

That sweet exterior you look at everyday
Is going to look the other way
You're causing me to want to stray

The love I said I had for you
Has left me playing the fool
But I always keep my cool

These childish games are going to get you nowhere
Because pretty soon I'll have you out my hair

A woman like me is hard to come by
You won't find another me
no matter how hard you try

So, bye-bye baby
Keep getting high now baby
That's all your good for
So, I'm walking out the door

I Hate Cake...

As a Child...
I Hate cake
All my parents do is bake
I want to play
But, "Not Now!" they say
I'm proud of what they do
But I need attention too

As a teen...
Ughhh, If I see another cake
Cake, Cake, Cake, for goodness sake
I don't want to help out
That's not what my life's about
I want to have fun
Sometimes I just want to run

As a young adult...
Wow my parent's work hard
I see that now
They did it for us,
to take over the business, wow

As an adult...
I didn't understand when I was younger
So, I thought I hated cake
But now that I've grown,
I can truly say,
I love my family in every way and
I do love Cake!!

What Is Love?

WHAT IS LOVE?
IS IT HAPPINESS OR HEARTACHE?
IS IT REAL OR IS IT FAKE?

IS IT PASSION RUN WILD?
OR THE UNCONDITIONAL FEELINGS
BETWEEN A PARENT AND CHILD?

THE MEANING OF LOVE
FOREVER A MYSTERY
IT'S BEEN THAT WAY
SINCE THE BEGINNING OF HISTORY.

LOVE TO ME IS A WARM SENSATION IN MY SOUL,
A FEELING I'LL CHERISH 'TILL THE DAY I GROW OLD.

THE MEANING OF LOVE
I STILL HAVEN'T A CLUE.

SO, I ASK YOU THIS QUESTION:
WHAT'S LOVE TO YOU?

Burning Desire

The fire inside me is
slowly consuming my every thought
Irrationalizing my sensibility,
causing me to feel distraught

I need you to heal me, caress me and feel me
To hold me tightly and tell me you want me
Extinguish my flames which are burning intensely
Only you know the way to caress me and bless me

I want you to undress me first with your eyes
Then remove all my clothing and open my thighs
I want to feel your lips moisten
every inch of my flesh
I want to feel your body on mine 'til we mesh

I want to feel your manhood deep inside
While I climb on top and give you a ride

I want to feel the moisture flow through our pores
As we share the hot, steamy passion
we've been longing for

Tell me my sweet, Do you feel the heat?
Will you put out my fire the way I desire?
Will you hold me until I melt in your arms?
Will you undress me gently and do me no harm?

Will you have my body writhing in ecstasy?
Will you fulfill my deepest desires and fantasies?

The desire I have for you is so strong
So baby, don't make me wait too long

You won't want our night to ever end
Signed your lover and special friend

Rise Phoenix, Rise!

I KNOW YOU'VE BEEN HURT
BEEN AFRAID
FELT LIKE DIRT
TAKEN ADVANTAGE OF AND BETRAYED
LEFT ALONE AND DISMAYED

RISE PHOENIX, RISE
FROM THE ASHES OF YOUR PAIN

RISE PHOENIX, RISE
LEAVE THE PAST FOR A NEW LIFE TO CLAIM

A LIFE FULL OF JOY
A LIFE FULL OF LOVE
A LIFE FREE OF SORROW
A GIFT FROM ABOVE

RISE PHOENIX, RISE
YOU ARE BORN AGAIN RENEWED
YOU GAINED LOTS OF STRENGTH
FROM ALL YOU'VE BEEN THROUGH

SPREAD YOUR WINGS AND SOAR FREE
FLY THROUGH THE SKY AND BE ALL YOU CAN BE

RISE PHOENIX, RISE!

Lotus;

Your Story's not over
How do I know?
Welcome to the Melody Show...

I suffered physical and emotional abuse
throughout my childhood
I was bullied, used, and misunderstood
I had many great memories but also many bad
My teenage years were particularly sad

My mom was on drugs and very abusive
I grew up with fear and resentment
and didn't want to live

I was sexually abused, and no one believed me
My self-esteem diminished and I didn't think clearly

I was a "chronic runaway" and felt so alone
I had no real place to call home
I trusted many people and wound up distraught
I dyed my hair and kept running
so, I wouldn't get caught

Of course, my "street life" didn't last very long
I was forced to go back to a dysfunctional life
and a mom who could never do wrong

I tried to move on and be a normal teen
but I was always depressed,
and my pain remained unseen

I met someone, moved out and had my first child
Seeing him was the first time in a while
that I had a genuine smile

But my home life was destroyed by drugs yet again
This time it was my baby daddy, my man
Again, I had to deal with mood swings & verbal abuse
all because of another loved one's drug use

I HAD TO LIVE IN A SHELTER TO ESCAPE ALL THE DRAMA
I DID ALL I COULD TO BE A GOOD MAMA

I LOST MY SON TO THE SYSTEM
BECAUSE THEY THOUGHT I COULDN'T DO IT
BUT THEY DIDN'T REALIZE I WAS A FIGHTER
AND WOULD NEVER QUIT

THEY GAVE ME AN ULTIMATUM
AND TRIED TO TAKE HIM AWAY
BUT I FOUGHT AND I CRIED FOR HIM,
I NEEDED HIM TO STAY

I WAS DETERMINED AND KNEW THAT HE NEEDED ME TOO
SO, I DID EVERYTHING A GOOD MOTHER WOULD DO
I GOT MYSELF TOGETHER AND VISITED HIM EVERY DAY
AND GUESS WHAT I GOT HIM BACK
AND NO ONE HAD ANYTHING TO SAY

EVENTUALLY, I MOVED ON AND MET SOMEONE NEW,
BUT LITTLE DID I KNOW, WE WOULD GO THROUGH HELL TOO

YEARS OF HIGHS AND LOWS
KICKED MY DEPRESSION IN FULL GEAR
I WAS LIED TO, CHEATED ON, & EMOTIONALLY
AND **PHYSICALLY** ABUSED YEAR AFTER YEAR.

I CONTEMPLATED SUICIDE TO END MY PAIN,
BUT I KNEW IF I DID
MY CHILDREN WOULD NEVER BE THE SAME

I FOUND THE STRENGTH TO LET GO
AND OPEN MY HEART
I MET SOMEONE NEW
WITH MY BEST INTEREST AT HEART

I FOUND THE SUPPORT THAT I WAS LACKING
FOR SO MANY YEARS
I FINALLY LEARNED HOW TO CONQUER MY FEARS

HE LOVES ALL OF ME
MY FLAWS AND ALL
I AM FINALLY HAPPY
GOD ANSWERED MY CALL

JUST LIKE THE LOTUS FLOWER,
I HAVE GAINED MY POWER...

I GREW BEAUTIFUL AND STRONG
DESPITE ALL THE DARKNESS, DIRT AND GRIME
I'M WRITING MORE CHAPTERS IN THIS BOOK CALLED LIFE
BECAUSE NOW IS MY TIME!

MY PASSION FOR LIFE HAS RETURNED
AND LOOK AT ME NOW

I AM A PHENOMENAL WIFE, MOTHER, AND
ENTREPRENEUR, WOW!!!!

Empowerment through compassion
That is the mission
From the darkness and pain
The sunshine will burn though
And enlighten your vision

You must learn from the things
that darken your days

To grow stronger within and help brighten the way
Reach out to others in your time of despair
they're there to help your heart & soul repair

Your story is not over,
There's so much more to be written
Your potential is limitless
So, don't keep it hidden

Rise from the ashes
Grow through the dirt
Fill your emptiness with strength
And put in the work

Replace your .
With a ;
And start a new chapter
Your story is not over
ETC;

ABOUT THE AUTHOR

Latina Celebrity Cake Artist, Melody Denise Velez, was born and raised in the Highbridge section of the Bronx in New York City. She currently resides in the Bronx, with her husband and two of their six children. Mrs. Velez fondly refers to her family as "The Puerto Rican Brady Bunch", since they have a blended family of three girls and three boys.

She studied at John Jay College of Criminal Justice before continuing her education in Forensic Psychology at Monroe College. Melody has a strong artistic background as well and loves to paint and write poetry. She has a passion for all things artistic, so watching cake shows on the Food Network and the Cooking Channel inspired her to experiment with cake design for her own family. Her friends and family began requesting that she bake cakes for their special engagements. Before she knew it, her business had begun.

Over the course of the next several years, Mrs. Velez's career proved to be a whirlwind for the ambitious, hard-driving cake artist. She proudly proclaims that she has a niche for listening to her client's needs and wishes. She is known for making her client's dreams come to life through her cake masterpieces, no matter how difficult the request or task at hand.

Melody states that a key defining moment in her career was when one of her clients cried with happiness when she had made her daughter so happy after she had struggled with depression for many months. Mrs. Velez reflects on that moment fondly stating, "I realized at that moment that I was doing more than baking and designing cake, I was creating memories and bringing joy to people that may not have those precious moments in their life."

Melody will continue expanding her impressive client list and her brand by exploring her ever evolving creative talents. She will focus on telling her story on multiple outlets and channels in the digital sector to inspire others to follow their dreams and make a positive change in society.

Melody D. Velez received a Power of Influence Award for her mental health advocacy. She is the co-founder of Lotus Flower, ETC Foundation and an advocate of Breaking the Stigmas associated with Mental Health Issues. She is a longtime sufferer of depression and struggles at times with keeping her depression at bay. She tells her story to encourage others to speak their truth, since so many people in urban communities feel ashamed to speak about their battles with mental health. Her goal is to teach people how to use artistic expressions as a means of art therapy to help cope with some of the everyday issues that affect mental health and well-being.

Melody is using her skills in creating cake art, to provide dream cakes for terminally ill children through an organization called Icing Smiles. She is also currently developing a program through her foundation where she can provide terminally ill youth with an entire birthday or prom experience using her resources in the entertainment industry.

Sharing her journey is something she is very passionate about and is the driving force behind this book. She plans on continuing to share her Life in Poetry with subsequent books and public speaking engagements.

Be Inspired

JOT DOWN YOUR THOUGHTS, WRITE YOUR OWN POEMS OR DOODLE AND DRAW. RELEASE YOUR STRESS & ANXIETY USING A PEN AND PAPER.

INSTEAD OF LASHING OUT VERBALLY OR PHYSICALLY TO A FRIEND, STRANGER OR LOVED ONE; LASH OUT ON THESE PAGES. I PROMISE IT WILL BE THERAPEUTIC!

_____

_____

_____

_____

_____

_____

_____

_____

_____

_____

_____

_____

_____

_____

_____

_____

_____

_____

_____

_____

_____

_____

_____

_____

_____

_____

_____

_____

_____

_____

_____

_____

_____

_____

_____

_____

_____

_____

_____

_____

Made in the USA
Middletown, DE
18 July 2024

57575441R00024